The Rourke Guide
to State Symbols

STATE SONGS

George Travis

The Rourke Press, Inc.
Vero Beach, Florida 32964

PHOTO CREDITS: Cover photo courtesy of Corel

COVER ILLUSTRATION: Jim Spence

CREATIVE SERVICES:
East Coast Studios, Merritt Island, Florida

EDITORIAL SERVICES:
Janice L. Smith for Penworthy

Library of Congress Cataloging-in-Publication Data

Travis, George, 1961-
   State songs / George Travis
      p. cm. — (The Rourke guide to state symbols)
   Song texts without the music
   Includes index.
   Summary: Gives the text and a brief history of all fifty state songs.
   ISBN 1-57103-299-1
   1. State songs—United States Texts Juvenile literature. [1. State songs.
2. Songs.] I. Title. II. Series.
ML54.6.T775S73 1999 <Case>
782.42'1599'0973—dc21   99-31933
                                               CIP

Printed in the USA

TABLE OF CONTENTS

INTRODUCTION

Patriotic songs express pride in certain places, especially countries and states. These kinds of songs have helped to boost spirits during hard times or celebrate success during good times.

You probably know "The Star-Spangled Banner." This is the official song, or national anthem, of the United States. Professional sports games and many public ceremonies begin with someone singing "The Star-Spangled Banner." To show your patriotism during the national anthem, you should face the nearest U.S. flag, take off your hat and place your right hand over your heart.

Each state has also adopted an official song. You can learn a lot about a state from the words, or lyrics, of its song. Many lyrics describe the state's scenery. Some honor the state's role in a war, such as the American Revolution or the Civil War. Other lyrics simply tell about the singer's pride.

State legislators make their state songs official by passing laws, although a few states have simply "adopted" their songs. Citizens have also voted to decide their official song. States may change their official songs at any time, however. Every effort has been made to present current information here about the honored songs.

Discover the deep pride Americans feel for their home states by reading or, even better, by singing these beloved songs.

ALABAMA

"Alabama"

Alabama, Alabama
We will aye be true to thee,
From thy Southern shores where groweth
By the sea thy orange tree
To thy Northern vale where floweth,
Deep blue the Tennessee
Alabama, Alabama, we will aye be true to thee.

Broad thy stream whose name thou bearest,
Grand thy Bigbee rolls along
Fair thy Coosa-Tallapoosa,
Bold thy Warrior dark and strong.
Goodlier than the land that Moses
Climbed lone Nebb's Mount to see.
Alabama, Alabama, we will aye be true to thee.

continued...

Brave and pure thy men and women,
Better this than corn and wine
Make us worthy, God in Heaven
Of this goodly land of Thine.
Hearts as open as thy doorways.
Liberal hands and spirits free.
Alabama, Alabama, we will aye be true to thee.

Little, little can I give thee,
Alabama, mother mine.
But that little—hand, brain, spirit.
All I have and am are thine.
Take, O take, the gift and giver.
Take and serve thyself with me.
Alabama, Alabama, we will aye be true to thee.

Written by Julia S. Tutwiler
Composed by Edna Gockel Gussen

Hard times had fallen on Alabama when Julia S. Tutwiler wrote this song. She hoped her words would help people feel proud of their homeland. Music by Edna Gockel Gussen replaced the first tune. In 1931, the state officially adopted the music and lyrics.

ALASKA

"Alaska's Flag"

Eight stars of gold on a field of blue—
Alaska's flag. May it mean to you
The blue of the sea, the evening sky,
The mountain lakes, and the flow'rs nearby;
The gold of the early sourdough's dreams,
The precious gold of the hills and streams;
The brilliant stars in the northern sky,
The "Bear"—the "Dipper"—and, shining high,
The great North Star with its steady light,
Over land and sea a beacon bright.
Alaska's flag—to Alaskans dear,
The simple flag of a last frontier.

Written by Marie Drake
Composed by Elinor Dusenbury

A teenager named Bennie Benson created Alaska's state flag in 1926. His beautiful design inspired Marie Drake to explain what the blue field and gold stars mean to Alaskans. Her worlds also paint a vivid picture of the state's grand landscape.

"Arizona"

Come to this land of sunshine
To this land where life is young.
Where the wide, wide world is waiting,
The songs that will now be sung.
Where the golden sun is flaming
Into warm, white shining day,
And the sons of men are blazing
Their priceless right of way.

Come stand beside the rivers
Within our valley broad.
Stand here with heads uncovered,
In the presence of our God!
While all around, about us
The brave, unconquered band,
As guardians and landmarks
The giant mountains stand.

continued...

Not alone for gold and silver
Is Arizona great.
But with graves of heroes sleeping,
All the land is consecrate!
O, come and live beside us
However far ye roam
Come and help us build up temples
And name those temples "home."

CHORUS
Sing the song that's in your hearts
Sing of the great Southwest,
Thank God, for Arizona
In splendid sunshine dressed.
For thy beauty and thy grandeur,
For thy regal robes so sheen
We hail thee Arizona
Our goddess and our queen.

Written by Margaret Rowe Clifford
Composed by Maurice Blumenthal

These lyrics speak of Arizona's many colorful landscapes. Known as the "Grand Canyon State," Arizona holds this national landmark in its northern plateau region. Mountains in the central area help create the sunny Sonoran Desert in the south.

ARKANSAS

"Arkansas" (You Run Deep in Me)

October morning in the Ozark Mountains,
Hills ablazing like that sun in the sky.
I fell in love there and the fire's still burning
A flame that never will die.

CHORUS
Oh, I may wander, but when I do
I will never be far from you.
You're in my blood and I know you'll always be.
Arkansas, you run deep in me.

Moonlight dancing on a delta levee,
To a band of frogs and whippoorwill
I lost my heart there one July evening
And it's still there, I can tell.

(CHORUS)

continued...

Magnolia blooming, Mama smiling,
Mallards sailing on a December wind.
God bless the memories I keep recalling
Like an old familiar friend.

(CHORUS)

And there's a river rambling through the fields
and valleys,
Smooth and steady as she makes her way south,
A lot like the people whose name she carries.
She goes strong and she goes proud.

Written by Wayland Holyfield

The state's 1987 General Assembly adopted "Arkansas" as an official state song. "Oh, Arkansas," written by Terry Rose and Gary Klaff, is also an official state song. Both songs show pride in the state's natural beauty.

CALIFORNIA

"I Love You California"

I love you California . . . you're the greatest state of all . . .
I love you in the winter, summer, spring, and in the fall.
I love your fertile valleys, your dear mountains I adore.
I love your grand old ocean and I love her rugged shore.

CHORUS
When the snow crowned Golden Sierras, Keep their watch o'er the valleys bloom.
It is there I would be in our land by the sea, Every breeze bearing rich perfume.
It is here nature gives of her rarest. It is Home Sweet Home to me.
And I know when I die I shall breathe my last sigh, For my sunny California.

I love your redwood forests—love your fields of yellow grain.
I love your summer breezes, and I love your winter rain.
I love you, land of flowers; land of honey, fruit and wine.
I love you, California; you have won this heart of mine.

I love your old gray Missions—love your vineyards stretching far.
I love you, California, with your Golden Gate ajar.
I love your purple sunsets, love your skies of azure blue.
I love you, California; I just can't help loving you.

I love you, Catalina—you are very dear to me.
I love you, Tamalpais, and I love Yosemite.
I love you, Land of Sunshine.
Half your beauties are untold.
I loved you in my childhood, and I'll love you when I'm old.

Written by F. B. Silverwood
Composed by A. F. Frankenstein

As early as 1915, "I Love You, California" had gained popularity at home and abroad. It even played on the first ship to sail the Panama Canal. The State Legislature named it as the state song in 1951. However, the honor didn't become law until 1988.

COLORADO

"Where the Columbines Grow"

Where the snowy peaks gleam in the moonlight,
Above the dark forests of pine,
And the wild foaming waters dash onward,
Toward lands where the tropic stars shine;
Where the scream of the bold mountain eagle
Responds to the notes of the dove
Is the purple robed West, the land that is best,
The pioneer land that we love.

CHORUS
Tis the land where the columbines grow,
Overlooking the plains far below,
While the cool summer breeze in
the evergreen trees
Softly sings where the columbines grow.

The bison is gone from the upland,
The deer from the canyon has fled,
The home of the wolf is deserted,
The antelope moans for his dead,
The war whoop re-echoes no longer,
The Indian's only a name,
And the nymphs of the grove in
their loneliness rove,
But the columbine blooms just the same.

continued...

Let the violet brighten the brookside,
In sunlight of earlier spring,
Let the fair clover bedeck the green meadow,
In days when the orioles sing,
Let the golden rod herald the autumn,
But, under the midsummer sky,
In its fair Western home, may the columbine
bloom
Till our great mountain rivers run dry.

Written by A. J. Fynn
Music by A. J. Fynn

The dainty but hearty Rocky Mountain Columbine, chosen as the state flower in 1899, inspired these lyrics. The General Assembly adopted "Where the Columbines Grow" as the official state song on May 8, 1915.

CONNECTICUT

"Yankee Doodle"

Yankee Doodle went to town,
Riding on a pony,
Stuck a feather in his hat,
And called it macaroni.

CHORUS
Yankee Doodle keep it up,
Yankee Doodle dandy,
Mind the music and the step,
And with the folks be handy.

Nearly all American children learn this happy tune. In Connecticut, it brings to mind the state's colonial history. The legislature there adopted "Yankee Doodle" as the state song in 1978.

DELAWARE

"Our Delaware"

Oh the hills of dear New Castle,
and the smiling vales between,
When the corn is all in tassel,
And the meadowlands are green;

Where the cattle crop the clover,
And its breath is in the air,
While the sun is shining over
Our beloved Delaware.

CHORUS
Oh our Delaware!
Our beloved Delaware!
For the sun is shining over
our beloved Delaware,
Oh our Delaware
Our beloved Delaware!
Here's the loyal son that pledges,
Faith to good old Delaware.

Where the wheat fields break and billow,
In the peaceful land of Kent,
Where the toiler seeks his pillow,
With the blessings of content;

continued...

Where the bloom that tints the peaches,
Cheeks of merry maidens share,
And the woodland chorus preaches
A rejoicing Delaware.

Dear old Sussex visions linger,
Of the holly and the pine,
Of Henlopen's jeweled finger,
Flashing out across the brine;

Of the gardens and the hedges,
And the welcome waiting there,
For the loyal son that pledges
Faith to good old Delaware.

From New Castle's rolling meadows,
Through the fair rich fields of Kent,
To the Sussex shores hear echoes,
Of the pledge we now present;

Liberty and Independence,
We will guard with loyal care,
And hold fast to freedom's presence,
In our home state Delaware.

Written by George B. Hynson
Composed by Will M. S. Brown

Delaware is divided into only three counties: New Castle, Kent and Sussex. George B. Hynson wrote a verse for each county in his poem, "Our Delaware." The fourth verse, written by Donn Devine, pledges loyalty to the state.

FLORIDA

"The Swanee River" (Old Folks at Home)

Way down upon de Swanee Ribber,
Far, far away,
Dere's wha my heart is turning ebber,
Dere's wha de old folks stay.
All up and down de whole creation
Sadly I roam,
Still longing for de old plantation,
And for de old folks at home.

CHORUS
All de world am sad and dreary,
Eb-rywhere I roam;
Oh, darkeys, how my heart grows weary,
Far from de old folks at home!

continued...

All round de little farm I wandered
When I was young,
Den many happy days I squandered,
Many de songs I sung.
When I was playing wid my brudder
Happy was I;
Oh, take me to my kind old mudder!
Dere let me live and die.

One little hut among de bushes,
One dat I love
Still sadly to my memory rushes,
No matter where I rove.
When will I see de bees a-humming
All round de comb?
When will I hear de banjo strumming,
Down in my good old home?

Written by Stephen C. Foster

In 1913, "Florida, My Florida" became the state song. Sixteen years later, legislators replaced the first official song with "The Swanee River." Stephen C. Foster, a popular American composer, reportedly wrote the tune in 1851 without ever visiting Florida.

GEORGIA

"Georgia on My Mind"

Melodies bring memories
That linger in my heart
Make me think of Georgia
Why did we ever part?

Some sweet day when blossoms fall
And all the world's a song
I'll go back to Georgia
'Cause that's where I belong.

Georgia, Georgia, the whole day through
Just an old sweet song keeps Georgia on my mind.
Georgia, Georgia, a song of you
Comes as sweet and clear as moonlight through the pines.

Other arms reach out to me
Other eyes smile tenderly
Still in peaceful dreams I see
The road leads back to you.

Georgia, Georgia, no peace I find
Just an old sweet song keeps Georgia on my mind.

Written by Stuart Gorrell
Composed by Hoagy Carmichael

Singer Ray Charles, a native of Georgia, sang this 1922 song for the Georgia Senate and House of Representatives in March of 1979. One month later, legislators chose it as the official state song. The song's title even appears on Georgia license plates!

HAWAII

Hawaii Ponoi

Hawaii ponoi Nana i kou, moi
Kalani Alii, ke Alii.
Makua lani e Kamehameha e
Na kaua e pale Me ka ihe.

(translation)
Hawaii's own true sons, be loyal to your chief
Your country's liege and lord, the sovereign
Father above us all, King
Who guarded in the war with his spear

Written by King David Kalakaua
Music by Prof. Henry Berger, the Royal
Bandmaster

The song first served as the Kingdom of Hawaii's national anthem. Hawaii kept "Hawaii Ponoi" as the official song when it became a U.S. territory in 1900 and through statehood in 1959.

IDAHO

"Here We Have Idaho"

And here we have Idaho—Winning her
way to fame,
Silver and gold in the sunlight blaze, and
romance in her name.

Singing, we're singing of you, ah, proudly too,
all our lives thru,
We'll go singing, singing of you, singing of Idaho.

continued...

You've heard of the wonders our
land does possess,
It's beautiful valleys and hills, The majestic
forests where nature abounds,
We love every nook and rill.

There's truly one state in this great land of ours
Where ideals can be realized
The pioneers made it so for you and me
A legacy we'll always prize.

Written by McKinley Helm & Albert J. Tompkins
Composed by Sallie Hume-Douglas

"Here We Have Idaho" came from the University of Idaho's song, "Our Idaho." The popular tune became the official state song in 1931.

ILLINOIS

"Illinois"

By thy rivers gently flowing, Illinois, Illinois,
O'er thy prairies verdant growing, Illinois, Illinois,
Comes an echo on the breeze.
Rustling through the leafy trees, and its mellow tones are these, Illinois, Illinois,
And its mellow tones are these, Illinois.

From a wilderness of prairies, Illinois, Illinois,
Straight thy way and never varies, Illinois, Illinois,
Till upon the inland sea,
Stands thy great commerical tree, turning all the world to thee, Illinois, Illinois,
Turning all the world to thee, Illinois.

When you heard your country calling, Illinois, Illinois,
Where the shot and shell were falling, Illinois, Illinois,
When the Southern host withdrew,
Pitting Gray against the Blue, There were none more brave than you, Illinois, Illinois,
There were none more brave than you, Illinois.

Not without thy wondrous story, Illinois, Illinois,
Can be writ the nation's glory, Illinois, Illinois,
On the record of thy years,
Abraham Lincoln's name appears, Grant and Logan, and our tears, Illinois, Illinois,
Grant and Logan, and our tears, Illinois.

Written by C.H. Chamberlain
Composed by Archibald Johnston

The 54th General Assembly passed a law making "Illinois" the state song. The lyrics show that Illinois takes great pride in Abraham Lincoln's legacy and the state's role in the Civil War.

INDIANA

"On the Banks of the Wabash, Far Away"

'Round my Indiana homesteads wave the cornfields,
In the distance loom the woodlands clear and cool.
Oftentimes my thoughts revert to scenes of childhood,
Where I first received my lessons, nature's school.
But one thing there is missing in the picture,
Without her face it seems so incomplete.
I long to see my mother in the doorway,
As she stood there years ago, her boy to greet.

CHORUS
Oh, the moonlight's fair tonight along the Wabash,
From the fields there comes the breath of newmown hay.
Through the sycamores the candle lights are gleaming,
On the banks of the Wabash, far away.

Many years have passed since I strolled by the river,
Arm in arm, with sweetheart Mary by my side,
It was there I tried to tell her that I loved her,
It was there I begged of her to be my bride.
Long years have passed since I strolled thro' there churchyard.
She's sleeping there, my angel, Mary dear,
I loved her, but she thought I didn't mean it,
Still I'd give my future were she only here.

Written by Paul Dresser
Composed by Paul Dresser

The Wabash River runs across Indiana and along the state's western border. This key waterway and the rolling countryside add charm to the song's tale of a lost love. The General Assembly adopted Paul Dresser's tune as the official state song in 1913.

IOWA

"Iowa State Song"

You asked what land I love the best, Iowa, tis Iowa.
The fairest State of all the west, Iowa, O! Iowa,
From yonder Mississippi's stream to where Missouri's waters gleam
O! fair it is as a poet's dream, Iowa, in Iowa.

See yonder fields of tasseled corn, Iowa in Iowa.
Where plenty fills her golden horn, Iowa in Iowa.
See how her wonderous prairies shine.
To yonder sunset's purpling line.
Of happy land, Of land of mine, Iowa, O! Iowa.

And she has made whose laughing eyes, Iowa, O! Iowa.
To him whose loves were Paradise. Iowa, O! Iowa
O! happiest fate that e'er was known.
Such eyes to shine for one alone.
To call such beauty all his own. Iowa, O! Iowa

Go read the story of thy past. Iowa, O! Iowa
What glorious deeds, what fame thou hast! Iowa, O! Iowa
So long as time's great cycle runs.
Or nations weep their fallen ones
Thou'll not forget thy patrial sons. Iowa, O! Iowa

Written by S.H.M. Byers

While imprisoned during the Civil War, Major S.H.M. Byers heard "My Maryland" sung in taunting tones by Confederate soldiers. He wanted Iowa to have a song honoring the state's rich farmland and loyal patriots, and he wrote this tribute in 1897. Like Maryland's song, Iowas's is sung to the tune "O, Tannenbaum."

KANSAS

"Home on the Range"

Oh, give me a home, where the buffalo roam,
Where the deer and the antelope play,
Where seldom is heard a discouraging word,
And the skies are not cloudy all day.

CHORUS
Home, home on the range,
Where the deer and the antelope play,
Where seldom is heard a discouraging word,
And the sky is not cloudy all day.

Written by Brewster Higley
Composed by Daniel Kelley

Dr. Brewster Higley wrote "Home on the Range" in a cabin near Smith Center in Kansas. Legislators made it the official state song in 1947. Almost all of Kansas remains as "range" or fields today, and the skies are sunny all day more than half of the year.

KENTUCKY

"My Old Kentucky Home"

The sun shines bright in the old Kentucky home
'tis summer, the people are gay,
the corn top's ripe and the
meadow's in the bloom
while the birds make music all the day.
The young folks roll on the little cabin floor
all merry, all happy, and bright.
By'n by hard times comes
a-knocking at the door,
then my old Kentucky home, good night.

CHORUS
Weep no more, my lady,
oh weep no more today.
We will sing our song for the old
Kentucky home,
for the old Kentucky home far away.

continued...

They hunt no more for the 'possum and the coon
on meadow, the hill and the shore.
They sing no more by the glimmer of the moon
on the bench by that old cabin door.
The day goes by like a shadow o'er the heart
with sorrow where all was delight.
The time has come when the people have to part
then my old Kentucky home, good night.

The head must bow and the back
will have to bend
wherever the people may go.
A few more days and the trouble all will end
in the field where sugar-canes may grow.
A few more days for to tote the weary load.
No matter, 'twill never be light.
A few more days till we totter on the road,
then my old Kentucky home, good night.

Written by Stephen C. Foster
Music by Stephen C. Foster

Stephen C. Foster wrote many popular and patriotic songs. Born on the Fourth of July, 1826, Foster composed more than 200 songs before he died in 1864. Scholars believe he wrote "My Old Kentucky Home" in 1853.

LOUISIANA

"Give Me Louisiana"

Give me Louisiana,
The State where I was born
The State of snowy cotton,
The best I've ever known;
A State of sweet magnolias,
And Creole melodies.

Oh give me Louisiana,
The State where I was born

Written by Doralice Fontane
Composed by Dr. John Croom

continued...

Oh what sweet old mem'ries
The mossy old oaks bring.

It brings us the story
of our Evangeline.

A State of old tradition,
of old plantation days
Makes good ole Louisiana
The sweetest of all States.

In 1970 and 1977, the legislature named "Give Me Louisiana" the official state song. The popular song "You Are My Sunshine" is also thought of as a state song.

MAINE

"State of Maine Song"

Grand State of Maine
Proudly we sing
to tell your glories to the land,
to shout your praises till the echoes ring.
Should fate unkind send us to roam
The scent of the fragrant pines,
the tang of the salty sea will call us home.

continued...

Oh, Pine Tree State
Your woods, fields and hills,
Your lakes, streams and rockbound coast
will ever fill our hearts with thrills
And tho' we seek far and wide
Our search will be in vain
To find a fairer spot on earth
than Maine! Maine! Maine!

Written by Roger Vinton Snow
Composed by Roger Vinton Snow

Adopted as the state song in 1937, "State of Maine Song" praises the natural beauty of this Atlantic-coast state.

21

MARYLAND

"Maryland My Maryland"

The despot's heel is on thy shore, Maryland!
His torch is at thy temple door, Maryland!
Avenge the patriotic gore That flecked the streets of Baltimore,
And be the battle queen of yore, Maryland! My Maryland!

Hark to an exiled son's appeal, Maryland!
My mother State! to thee I kneel, Maryland!
For life and death, for woe and weal, Thy peerless chivalry reveal,
And gird they beauteous limbs with steel, Maryland! My Maryland!

Thou wilt not cower in the dust, Maryland!
Thy beaming sword shall never rust, Maryland!
Remember Carroll's sacred trust, Remember Howard's warlike thrust,—
And all they slumberers with the just, Maryland! My Maryland!

Come! 'tis the red dawn of the day, Maryland!
Come with thy panoplied array, Maryland!
With Ringgold's spirit for the fray, With Watson's blood at Monterey,
With fearless Lowe and dashing May, Maryland! My Maryland!

Come! for thy shield is bright and strong, Maryland!
Come! for thy dalliance does thee wrong, Maryland!
Come to thine own heroic throng, Stalking with Liberty along,
And chaunt thy dauntless slogan song, Maryland! My Maryland!

Dear Mother! burst the tyrant's chain, Maryland!
Virginia should not call in vain, Maryland!
She meets her sisters on the plain—"Sic semper!" 'tis the proud refrain
That baffles minions back again, Maryland! My Maryland!

MARYLAND

"Maryland My Maryland"

continued...

I see the blush upon thy cheek, Maryland!
For thou wast ever bravely meek, Maryland!
But lo! there surges forth a shriek From hill to fill, from creek to creek—
Potomac calls to Chesapeake, Maryland! My Maryland!

Thou wilt not yield the vandal toll, Maryland!
Thou wilt not crook to his control, Maryland!
Better the fire upon thee roll, Better the blade, the shot, the bowl,
Than crucifixion of the soul, Maryland! My Maryland!

I hear the distant thunder-hum, Maryland!
The Old Line's bugle, fife, and drum, Maryland!
She is not dead, nor deaf, nor dumb—Huzza! she spurns the Northern scum!
She breathes! she burns! she'll come! she'll come! Maryland! My Maryland!

Written by James Ryder Randall

James Ryder Randall wrote his poem to honor Maryland and the South in 1861, just as the first battles of the Civil War began. The traditional song "O, Tannenbaum" provides the tune. Maryland made it the official state song in 1939.

MASSACHUSETTS

"All Hail to Massachusetts"

All hail to Massachusetts, the land of the free and the brave!
For Bunker Hill and Charlestown, and flag we love to wave;
For Lexington and Concord, and the shot heard 'round the world;
All hail to Massachusetts, we'll keep her flag unfurled.
She stands upright for freedom's light that shines from sea to sea;
All hail to Massachusetts! Our country 'tis of thee!

All hail to grand old Bay State, the home of the bean and the cod,
Where pilgrims found a landing and gave their thanks to God.
A land of opportunity in the good old U.S.A.
Where men live long and prosper, and people come to stay.
Don't sell her short but learn to court her industry and stride;
All hail to grand old Bay State! The land of pilgrim's pride!

All hail to Massachusetts, renowned in the Hall of Fame!
How proudly wave her banners emblazoned with her name!
In unity and brotherhood, sons and daughters go hand in hand;
All hail to Massachusetts, there is no finer land!
It's M-A-S-S-A-C-H-U-S-E-T-T-S.
All hail to Massachusetts! All hail! All hail! All hail!

Written by Arthur J. Marsh

The "shot heard 'round the world" started the American Revolution, a cornerstone of the state's long history. Massachusetts legislators adopted this proud song in 1966, but they did not make it the official state song until July of 1981.

MICHIGAN
"Michigan, My Michigan"

A song to thee, fair State of mine,
Michigan, my Michigan.
But greater song than this is thine,
Michigan, my Michigan.
The whisper of the forest tree.
The thunder of the inland sea;
Unite in one grand symphony
Of Michigan, my Michigan.

continued...

I sing a State of all the best,
Michigan, my Michigan;
I sing a State with riches bless'd
Michigan, my Michigan;
Thy mines unmask a hidden store,
But richer thy historic lore,
More great the love thy builders bore,
O Michigan, my Michigan.

Written by Douglas M. Malloch

Like the state songs of Maryland and Iowa, the state song of Michigan uses the melody of "O, Tannenbaum" for its patriotic words.

MINNESOTA
"Hail Minnesota"

Minnesota, hail to thee!
Hail to thee, our state so dear!
Thy light shall ever be
A beacon bright and clear,
Thy son and daughters true
will proclaim thee near and far,
They shall guard thy fame
And adore thy name,
Thou shalt be their Northern Star.

Like the stream that bends to sea,
Like the pine that seeks the blue,
Minnesota, still for thee,
Thy sons are strong and true,
From the woods and waters fair,
From the prairies waving fair,
At thy call they throng,
With their shout and song,
Hailing thee their Northern Star.

Two University of Minnesota students wrote this song in 1904 and 1905. Still sung at the University today, "Hail Minnesota" became the official state song in 1945.

MISSISSIPPI

"Go, Mississippi"

*States may sing their songs of praise
With waving flags and hip-hoo-rays,
Let cymbals crash and let bells ring
'Cause here's one song I'm proud to sing.*

*CHORUSES
Go, Mississippi, keep rolling along,
Go, Mississippi, you cannot go wrong,
Go, Mississippi, we're singing your song,
M-I-S-S-I-S-S-I-P-P-I*

*Go, Mississippi, you're on the right track,
Go, Mississippi, and this is a fact,
Go, Mississippi, you'll never look back,
M-I-S-S-I-S-S-I-P-P-I*

continued...

*Go, Mississippi, straight down the line,
Go, Mississippi, ev'rything's fine,
Go, Mississippi, it's your state and mine,
M-I-S-S-I-S-S-I-P-P-I*

*Go, Mississippi, continue to roll,
Go, Mississippi, the top is the goal,
Go, Mississippi, you'll have and you'll hold,
M-I-S-S-I-S-S-I-P-P-I*

*Go, Mississippi, get up and go,
Go, Mississippi, let the world know,
That our Mississippi is leading the show,
M-I-S-S-I-S-S-I-P-P-I*

Written by Houston Davis
Music by Houston Davis

"Go, Mississippi" is like a cheer for the entire state. Spelling the state's name in the chorus creates a bright rhythm that makes the song fun to sing for children and adults. The state adopted the song officially in 1962.

MISSOURI
"Missouri Waltz"

Hush-a-bye ma baby, slumber time is comin' soon.
Rest yo head upon my breast, while mommy hums a tune.
The sandman is calling, where shadows are falling,
While the soft breezes sigh as in days long gone by.

Way down in Missouri where I heard this melody,
When I was a little child on my mommy's knee.
The old folks were hummin',
Their banjos were strummin',
So sweet and low.

Strum, strum, strum, strum, strum,
Seems I hear those banjos playing once again,
Hum, hum, hum, hum, hum,
That same old plaintive strain.

Hear that mournful melody,
It just haunts you the whole day long.
And you wander in dreams,
Back to Dixie it seems
When you hear that old song.

Written by J. R. Shannon
Music by John Valentine Eppel as arranged by Frederick Knight Logan

The 1914 song "Missouri Waltz" didn't gain popularity until the early 1940s. When Missouri native Harry S. Truman became president in 1945, the song gained even more fans. The state made it the official song in 1949.

MONTANA

"Montana"

Tell me of that Treasure State
Story always new,
Tell of its beauties grand
And its hearts so true.

Mountains of sunset fire
The land I love the best
Let me grasp the hand of one
From out the golden West.

CHORUS:
Montana, Montana,
Glory of the West
Of all the states from coast to coast,
You're easily the best.
Montana, Montana,
Where skies are always blue
M-O-N-T-A-N-A,
Montana, I love you.

continued...

Each country has its flow'r;
Each one plays a part,
Each bloom brings a longing hope
To some lonely heart.

Bitter Root to me is dear
Growing in my land
Sing then that glorious air
The one I understand.

(CHORUS)

Written by Charles C. Cohan
Composed by Joseph E. Howard

In 1910, Charles C. Cohan and Joseph E. Howard wrote "Montana" one night during a theater party. Howard's traveling show performed it the next day. The crowd loved the song! This overnight sensation became the official state song in 1935.

NEBRASKA
"Beautiful Nebraska"

Beautiful Nebraska, peaceful prairieland,
laced with many rivers, and the hills of sand,
dark green valleys cradled in the earth,
rain and sunshine bring abundant birth.

CHORUS
Beautiful Nebraska, as you look around,
you will find a rainbow reaching to the ground.

continued...

All these wonders by the Master's hand,
Beautiful Nebraskaland.
We are so proud of this state where we live.
There is no place that has so much to give.

(CHORUS)

Written by Jim Fras

Lawmakers took several years to decide on a state song. They finally chose "Beautiful Nebraska" in 1967. Jim Fras wrote the song after he moved to Lincoln from Russia in 1952.

NEVADA
"Home Means Nevada"

Home means Nevada
Home means the hills.
Home means the sage and the pine
Out by the Truckee, silvery rills
Out where the sun always shines
Here is the land which I love the best
Fairer than all I can see
Deep in the heart of the golden west
Home means Nevada to me.

Written by Bertha Raffetto
Music by Bertha Raffetto

The Nevada legislature adopted "Home Means Nevada" as the official state song in 1933. Bertha Raffetto's words paint a colorful picture of the state's vast natural resources.

NEW HAMPSHIRE

"Old New Hampshire"

With a skill that knows no measure,
From the golden store of Fate
God, in His great love and wisdom,
Made the rugged Granite State;
Made the lakes, the fields, the forests;
Made the rivers and the rills;
Made the bubbling, crystal fountains
Of New Hampshire's Granite Hills

REFRAIN
Old New Hampshire, Old New Hampshire

Written by Dr. John F. Holmes
Composed by Maurice Hoffmann

continued...

Old New Hampshire Grand and Great
We will sing of Old New Hampshire,
Of the dear old Granite State

Builded He New Hampshire glorious
From the borders to the sea;
And with matchless charm and splendor
Blessed her for eternity.
Hers, the majesty of mountain;
Hers, the grandeur of the lake;
Hers, the truth as from the hillside
Whence her crystal waters break
(REFRAIN)

In 1977, legislators agreed to keep the 1926 tune "Old New Hampshire" as the official state song. They also named seven other "honorary" state songs. Today, the state has nine state songs!

NEW JERSEY

"I'm From New Jersey"

I'm from New Jersey and I'm proud about it,
I love the Garden State
I'm from New Jersey and I want to shout it,
I think it's simply great.
All of the other states throughout the nation,
may mean a lot to some;
But I wouldn't want another,
Jersey is like no other
I'm glad that's where I'm from.

Words by Red Mascara
Music by Red Mascara as arranged by Parke Frankenfield

The New Jersey coastline stretches 127 miles along the Atlantic Ocean, making the state a favorite of tourists. But, as this song shows, people who live in New Jersey love it best.

NEW MEXICO

"O, Fair New Mexico"

Kissed by the golden sunshine, is Nuevo Mejico.
Land of the Montezuma, with fiery hearts aglow,
Land of the deeds historic, is Nuevo Mejico.

CHORUS
Oh! Fair New Mexico, we love, we love you so,
Our hearts with pride o'er flow,
No matter where we go.
Oh! Fair New Mexico, we love, we love you so,
The grandest state we know—NEW MEXICO!

Written by Elizabeth Garrett

New Mexico became a state in 1912. Three years later, Elizabeth Garrett wrote this tribute to the 47th state. The legislature officially adopted the song in 1917.

NEW YORK

"I Love New York"

I LOVE NEW YORK
(repeat 3 times)

There isn't another like it.
No matter where you go.
And nobody can compare it.
It's win and place and show.

Written by Steve Karmen
Composed by Steve Karmen

continued...

New York is special.
New York is diff'rent 'cause there's no place else
on earth quite like New York and that's why

I LOVE NEW YORK
(repeat 3 times)

The state adopted "I Love New York" as the official state song in 1980. The song also supported the famous "I (Heart Symbol) New York" tourism campaign.

NORTH CAROLINA
"The Old North State"

Carolina! Carolina! heaven's blessings attend her,
While we live we will cherish, protect and defend her,
Tho' the scorner may sneer at and witlings defame her,
Still our hearts swell with gladness whenever we name her.

Hurrah! Hurrah! the Old North State forever,
Hurrah! Hurrah! the good Old North State.

Tho' she envies not others, their merited glory,
Say whose name stands the foremost, in liberty's story,
Tho' too true to herself e'er to crouch to oppression,
Who can yield to just rule a more loyal submission.

Hurrah! Hurrah! the Old North State forever,
Hurrah! Hurrah! the good Old North State.

Then let all those who love us, love the land that we live in,
As happy a region as on this side of heaven,
Where plenty and peace, love and joy smile before us,
Raise aloud, raise together the heart thrilling chorus.

Hurrah! Hurrah! the Old North State forever,
Hurrah! Hurrah! the good Old North State.

Written by William Gaston
Composed by Mrs. E. E. Randolph

The General Assembly of 1927 named "The Old North State" the official state song. This marked the first state symbol for the state; the legislators didn't name another state symbol until 1941.

"North Dakota Hymn"

North Dakota, North Dakota,
With thy prairies wide and free,
All thy sons and daughters love thee,
Fairest state from sea to sea;
North Dakota, North Dakota,
Here we pledge ourselves to thee.

Here thy loyal children singing,
Songs of happiness and praise,
Far and long the echoes ringing,
Through the vastness of thy ways;
North Dakota, North Dakota,
We will serve thee all our days.

continued...

Onward, onward, onward going,
Light of courage in thine eyes,
Sweet the winds above thee blowing,
Green thy fields and fair thy skies;
North Dakota, North Dakota,
Brave the soul that in thee lies.

God of freedom, all victorious,
Give us souls serene and strong,
Strength to make the future glorious,
Keep the echo of our song;
North Dakota, North Dakota,
In our hearts forever long.

Written by James W. Foley
Composed by Dr. C. S. Putnam

In 1926, poet James Foley answered an educator's request for a song about the state with "North Dakota Hymn." Dr. C. S. Putnam arranged the music. Twenty years after its first public performance, "North Dakota Hymn" became the official state song in 1947.

OHIO

"Beautiful Ohio"

I sailed away;
Wandered afar;
Crossed the mighty restless sea;
Looked for where I ought to be.
Cities so grand, mountains above,
Led to this land I love.

CHORUS
Beautiful Ohio, where the golden grain
Dwarf the lovely flowers in the summer rain.
Cities rising high, silhouette the sky.
Freedom is supreme in this majestic land;
Mighty factories seem to hum in tune, so grand.
Beautiful Ohio, thy wonders are in view,
Land where my dreams all come true!

Written by Ballard MacDonald with special lyrics by Wilbert B. McBride
Composed by Mary Earl

"Beautiful Ohio" became the official state song in 1969. The words written by Ballard MacDonald needed changes twenty years later, so the Ohio legislature adopted new lyrics written by a lawyer from Youngstown, Wilbert McBride.

OKLAHOMA

"Oklahoma"

Brand new state! Brand new state, gonna treat you great!
Gonna give you barley, carrots and pertaters,
Pasture fer the cattle, spinach and temayters!
Flowers on the prarie where the June bugs zoom,
Plen'y of air and plen'y of room,
Plen'y of room to swing a rope!
Plen'y of heart and plen'y of hope.

Oklahoma, where the wind comes sweepin' down the plain,
And the wavin' wheat can sure smell sweet
When the wind comes right behind the rain.
Oklahoma, ev'ry night my honey lamb and I
Sit alone and talk and watch a hawk makin' lazy circles in the sky.
We know we belong to the land
And the land we belong to is grand!
And when we say—Yeeow! A-yip-i-o-ee ay!
We're only sayin' You're doin' fine, Oklahoma! Oklahoma—O.K.

Written by Oscar Hammerstein II
Music by Richard Rodgers

The state's song came directly from the stage. The award-winning team of Oscar Hammerstein II and Richard Rodgers wrote "Oklahoma" for the musical of the same name. The Oklahoma legislature named it the state song in 1953.

OREGON

"Oregon, My Oregon"

Land of the Empire Builders,
Land of the Golden West;
Conquered and held by free men,
Fairest and the best.
On-ward and upward ever,
Forward and on, and on;
Hail to thee, Land of the Heroes, My Oregon.

Words by J. A. Buchanan
Music by Henry B. Murtagh

continued...

Land of the rose and sunshine,
Land of the summer's breeze;
Laden with health and vigor,
Fresh from the western seas.
Blest by the blood of martyrs,
Land of the setting sun;
Hail to thee, Land of Promise, My Oregon.

Written in 1920, "Oregon, My Oregon" won a statewide contest and gained popularity. Just seven years later, legislators made it the official state song.

PENNSYLVANIA

"Pennsylvania"

CHORUS
Pennsylvania, Pennsylvania,
May your future be,
filled with honor everlasting
as your history.

Pennsylvania, Pennsylvania,
Mighty is your name,
Steeped in glory and tradition,
Object of acclaim.
Where brave men fought the foe of freedom,

Written by Eddie Khoury and Ronnie Bonner
Composed by Eddie Khoury and Ronnie Bonner

continued...

Tyranny decried,
'Til the bell of independence
filled the countryside.

(CHORUS)
Pennsylvania, Pennsylvania,
Blessed by God's own hand,
Birthplace of a mighty nation,
Keystone of the land.
Where first our country's flag unfolded,
Freedom to proclaim,
May the voices of tomorrow
glorify your name.

The Commonwealth of Pennsylvania became a state in 1787. More than 203 years later, the legislature finally chose "Pennsylvania" as the official state song.

RHODE ISLAND

"Rhode Island It's for Me"

Rhode Island, oh, Rhode Island,
surrounded by the sea.
There's a place for everyone,
Rhode Island it's for me!

I've been to every state we have,
but I think I'm inclined
to say that Rhody stole my heart.
You can have the forty-nine.
Herring gulls that dot the sky,
blue waves that paint the rocks,
water rich with Neptune's life,
the boats that line the docks.
I see the lighthouse flickering
to help the sailors see.
There's a place for everyone,
Rhode Island it's for me.

continued...

I love the fresh October days,
the buzz on College Hill,
art that moves an eye to tear,
a jeweler's special skill.
Icicles refract from the sun,
snow falling gracefully.
Some search for a place that's warm,
Rhode Island it's for me!

The skyline piercing Providence,
the State House dome so rare.
Residents who speak their minds,
no longer unaware.
Roger Williams would be proud to see his colony,
so don't sell short this precious port.
Rhode Island it's for me!

Written by Charlie Hall

In July 1996, Rhode Island lawmakers adopted a new state song. "Rhode Island It's for Me" replaced "Rhode Island," which had been the official song for fifty years. The new song describes the state's scenery and reflects some of Rhode Island's colonial history.

SOUTH CAROLINA

"Carolina"

Hold up the glories of thy dead;
Say how thy elder children bled,
And point to Eutaw's battle-bed.
Carolina! Carolina!

Throw thy bold banner to the breeze!
Front with thy ranks the threatening seas
Like thine own proud armorial trees,
Carolina! Carolina!

Thy skirts indeed the foe may part,
Thy robe be pierced with sword and dart,
They shall not touch thy noble heart,
Carolina! Carolina!

Girt with such wills to do and bear,
Assured in right, and mailed in prayer,
Thou wilt not bow thee to despair,
Carolina! Carolina!

Written by Henry Timrod
Composed by Anne Custis Burgess

Henry Timrod, South Carolina's famous poet, wrote these lyrics to honor the state's soldiers. The General Assembly made "Carolina" the legal state song in 1911. In 1984, "South Carolina on My Mind" by Hank Martin and Buzz Arledge was also declared a state song.

SOUTH DAKOTA

"Hail! South Dakota!"

Hail! South Dakota, A great state of the land,
Health, wealth and beauty, That's what makes her grand;
She has her Black Hills, And mines with gold so rare,
And with her scenery, No other state can compare.

Come where the sun shines, And where life's worth your while,
You won't be here long, 'Till you'll wear a smile;
No state's so healthy, And no folk quite so true,
To South Dakota we welcome you.

Hail! South Dakota, The state we love the best,
Land of our fathers, Builders of the west;
Home of the Badlands, and Rushmore's ageless shrine,
Black Hills and prairies, Farmland and Sunshine.
Hills, farms and prairies, Blessed with bright Sunshine.

Written by DeeCort Hammitt
Composed by DeeCort Hammitt

"Hail! South Dakota!" became the official state song in 1943. Its words highlight many of South Dakota's famous places, such as the Black Hills, the Badlands and Mount Rushmore with its likeness of four presidents carved into the granite there.

TENNESSEE

"My Homeland, Tennessee"

O Tennessee, that gave us birth,
To thee our hearts bow down.
For thee our love and loyalty
Shall weave a fadeless crown.
Thy purple hills our cradle was;
Thy fields our mother breast
Beneath thy sunny bended skies,
Our childhood days were blessed.

Could we forget our heritage
Of heroes strong and brave?
Could we do aught but cherish it,
Unsullied to the grave?
Ah no! the State where Jackson sleeps,
Shall ever peerless be.
We glory in thy majesty;
Our homeland, Tennessee.

continued...

'Twas long ago our fathers came,
A free and noble band,
Across the mountain's frowning heights
To seek a promised land.
And here before their raptured eyes;
in beauteous majesty:
Outspread the smiling valleys
Of the winding Tennessee.

O Tennessee: Fair Tennessee:
Our love for thee can never die:
Dear homeland, Tennessee.

Written by Nell Grayson Taylor
Composed by Roy Lamont Smith

"My Homeland, Tennessee" became the state's first official song in 1925. Since then, Tennessee has named five more state songs. "Tennessee Waltz," one of the most famous of the songs honoring the state, was named an official state song in 1965.

TEXAS

"Texas, Our Texas"

Texas, Our Texas! all hail the mighty State!
Texas, Our Texas! so wonderful so great!
Boldest and grandest, withstanding ev'ry test
O Empire wide and glorious, you stand supremely blest.

(CHORUS)

Texas, O Texas! your freeborn single star,
Sends out its radiance to nations near and far,
Emblem of Freedom! it set our hearts aglow,
With thoughts of San Jacinto and glorious Alamo.

(CHORUS)

Texas, dear Texas! from tyrant grip now free,
Shines forth in splendor, your star of destiny!
Mother of heroes, we come your children true,
Proclaiming our allegiance, our faith, our love for you.

CHORUS
God bless you Texas! And keep you brave and strong,
That you may grow in power and worth, throughout the ages long.
God bless you Texas! And keep you brave and strong,
That you may grow in power and worth, throughout the ages long.

Written by William J. Marsh and Gladys Yoakum Wright
Composed by William J. Marsh

"Texas, Our Texas" won a statewide contest for a new state song. William J. Marsh of Fort Worth wrote the music and lyrics, with some help from Gladys Yoakum Wright. The legislature made it the official state song in 1929.

UTAH

"Utah, We Love Thee"

Land of the mountains high,
Utah, we love thee;
Land of the sunny sky,
Utah, we love thee;
Far in the glorious west,
Throned on the mountain's crest,
In robes of statehood dress'd,
Utah, we love thee.

Columbia's brighest star,
Utah, we love thee;
Thy lustre shines afar,
Utah, we love thee;
Bright in our banner's blue,
Among her sisters true,
She proudly comes to view,
Utah, we love thee.

Land of the Pioneers,
Utah, we love thee;
Grow with the coming years,
Utah, we love thee;
With wealth and peace in store,
To fame and glory soar,
God guarded evermore,
Utah, we love thee.

Written by Evan Stephens
Composed by Evan Stephens

In January of 1896, Evan Stephens brought together a chorus of 1,000 children to perform his song. It was the first of many performances of "Utah, We Love Thee," which became the official state song in 1917.

VERMONT

"Hail, Vermont"

Hail to Vermont!
Lovely Vermont!
Hail to Vermont so fearless!
Sing we a song!
Sing loud and long!
To our little state so peerless!
Green are her hills, Clear are her rills.
Fair are her lakes, and rivers and valleys;
Blue are her skies, Peaceful she lies,
But when roused to a call she speedily rallies
Hail to Vermont! Dear old Vermont!
Our love for you is so great.
We cherish your name,
We laud! We acclaim!
Our own Green Mountain State.

continued...

Proud of Vermont. Lovely Vermont,
Proud of her charm and her beauty;
Proud of her name, Proud of her fame,
We're proud of her sense of duty;
Proud of her past. Proud first and last.
Proud of her lands and proud of her waters.
Her men are true. Her women, too.
We're proud of her sons
and proud of her daughters
Hail to Vermont! Dear old Vemont!
Our love for you is great.
We cherish your name,
We laud! We acclaim!
Our own Green Mountain State.

Written by Josephine H. Perry
Music by Josephine H. Perry

"Hail, Vermont" became the state song in 1938. Fifty years later, legislators asked the Vermont Arts Council to help them find a "singable melody" for a new state song. People could vote on-line for their favorites. The winner will be announced July 15, 1999.

"Carry Me Back to Old Virginny"

Carry me back to old Virginny,
There's where the cotton and the corn and tatoes grow,
There's where the birds warble sweet in the springtime,
There's where the old darkey's heart am long'd to go,
There's where I labored so hard for old massa,
Day after day in the field of yellow corn,
No place on earth do I love more sincerely
Than old Virginny, the state where I was born.

CHORUS
Carry me back to old Virginny,
There's where the cotton and the corn and tatoes grow,
There's where the birds warble sweet in the springtime,
There's where this old darkey's heart am long'd to go.

Carry me back to old Virginny,
There let me live 'till I wither and decay,
Long by the old Dismal Swamp have I wandered,
There's where this old darkey's life will pass away.
Massa and missis have long gone before me,
Soon we will meet on that bright and golden shore,
There we'll be happy and free from all sorrow,
There's where we'll meet and we'll never part no more.

Written by James Bland

A black performer, James Bland, wrote "Carry Me Back to Old Virginny" in 1875. The song served as Virginia's official state song from 1940 to 1997. The Virginia Senate voted to retire the song in favor of finding a new tune with more modern lyrics.

WASHINGTON

"Washington, My Home"

This is my country;
God gave it to me;
I will protect it,
Ever keep it free.
Small towns and cities rest here in the sun,
Filled with our laughter.
Thy will be done.

(REFRAIN)
Washington my home; Where ever I may roam;
This is my land, my native land, Washington, my home.
Our verdant forest green, Caressed by silv'ry stream.
From mountain peak to fields of wheat, Washington, my home.
There's peace you feel and understand. In this, our own beloved land.
We greet the day with head held high, And forward ever is our cry.
We'll happy ever be as people always free.
For you and me a destiny; Washington my home.
For you and me a destiny; Washington my home.

Written by Helen Davis
Arranged by Stuart Churchill

In 1909, legislators noted "Washington Beloved" as a popular choice for the state song, but they failed to make it official. Fifty years later, legislators passed a law to make "Washington, My Home" the official state song.

WEST VIRGINIA

"West Virginia Hills"

Oh, the West Virginia hills! How majestic and how grand,
With their summits bathed in glory, Like our Prince Immanuel's Land!
Is it any wonder then, That my heart with rapture thrills,
As I stand once more with loved ones On those West Virginia hills?

CHORUS
Oh, the hills, beautiful hills, How I love those West Virginia hills!
If o'er sea o'er land I roam, Still I'll think of happy home,
And my friends among the West Virginia hills.

Oh, the West Virginia hills! Where my childhood hours were passed,
Where I often wandered lonely, And the future tried to cast;
Many are our visions bright, Which the future ne'er fulfills;
But how sunny were my daydreams On those West Virginia hills!

continued...

(CHORUS)

Oh, the West Virginia hills! How unchang'd they seem to stand,
With their summits pointed skyward To the Great Almighty's Land!
Many changes I can see, Which my heart with sadness fills;
But no changes can be noticed In those West Virginia hills.

(CHORUS)

Oh, the West Virginia hills! I must bid you now adieu.
In my home beyond the mountains I shall ever dream of you;
In the evening time of life, If my Father only wills,
I shall still behold the vision Of those West Virginia hills.

(CHORUS)

Words by Mrs. Ellen King,
Music by H. E. Engle

State lawmakers have chosen three official state songs since 1947. That year, "West Virginia, My Home Sweet Home" became the first official state song. In 1961, "The West Virginia Hills" joined the list, and two years later, "This Is My West Virginia" also gained the honor.

WISCONSIN

"On, Wisconsin!"

On, Wisconsin! On, Wisconsin!
Grand old badger state!
We, thy loyal sons and daughters,
Hail thee, good and great.
On, Wisconsin! On, Wisconsin!
Champion of the right,
"Forward", our motto
God will give thee might!

Written by J. S. Hubbard and Charles D. Rosa
Composed by William T. Purdy

"On, Wisconsin!" began as a football cheering song. First played in 1909 at the University of Wisconsin, the tune earned praise from famous band leader John Philip Sousa. In 1913, the words were changed to honor the state. Legislators adopted it as the official state song in 1959.

WYOMING

"Wyoming"

In the far and mighty West,
Where the crimson sun seeks rest,
There's a growing splendid State that lies above,
On the breast of this great land;
Where the massive Rockies stand,
There's Wyoming young and strong, the State I love!

CHORUS
Wyoming, Wyoming! Land of the sunlight clear!
Wyoming, Wyoming! Land that we hold so dear!
Wyoming, Wyoming! Precious art thou and thine!
Wyoming, Wyoming! Beloved State of mine!

In the flowers wild and sweet,
Colors rare and perfumes meet;
There's the columbine so pure, the daisy too,
Wild the rose and red it springs,
White the button and its rings,
Thou art loyal for they're red and white and blue,

continued...

Where thy peaks with crowned head,
Rising till the sky they wed,
Sit like snow queens ruling wood and stream and plain;
'Neath thy granite bases deep,
'Neath thy bosom's broadened sweep,
Lie the riches that have gained and brought thee fame.

Other treasures thou dost hold,
Men and women thou dost mould,
True and earnest are the lives that thou dost raise,
Strengthen thy children though dost teach,
Nature's truth thou givest to each,
Free and noble are thy workings and thy ways.

In the nation's banner free
There's one star that has for me
A radiance pure and splendor like the sun;
Mine it is, Wyoming's star,
Home it leads me near or far;
O Wyoming! All my heart and love you've won!

Written by C. E. Winter
Composed by G. E. Knapp

Wyoming lawmakers passed a law to make "Wyoming" the official state song in 1955. The song's many verses describe the mountain landscape, wild flowers and other treasures found in Wyoming.